ALSO BY FRANK MARESCA

With Roger Ricco and Julia Weissman
American Primitive: Discoveries in Folk Sculpture

$\mathcal{A}$
CERTAIN
STYLE

A CERTAIN STYLE

THE ART OF THE PLASTIC HANDBAG, 1949-59

SELECTED AND EDITED BY

ROBERT GOTTLIEB AND FRANK MARESCA

PHOTOGRAPHS BY

EDWARD SHOFFSTALL AND FRANK MARESCA

ALFRED A. KNOPF NEW YORK 1988

THIS IS A BORZOI BOOK
PUBLISHED BY ALFRED A. KNOPF, INC.

LIBRARY OF CONGRESS
CATALOGING-IN-PUBLICATION DATA

Gottlieb, Robert.
A certain style.
1. Plastic handbags—United States—Collectors
and collecting.   I. Maresca, Frank.   II. Title.
NK4890.H34G68   1988   685'.51   88-45340
ISBN 0-394-56893-1

Manufactured in Italy

FIRST EDITION

To Victoria, and to Maria (despite) and Lizzie (because)

A CERTAIN STYLE

Unknown maker, ca. 1920s, 4¹/₂″ W × 6¹/₄″ H × 1″ D.

INTRODUCTION

Toward the end of the 1940s, a relatively new material (plastic), a new technology for dealing with it, and a fresh (postwar) aesthetic led to a new version of an old artifact: the handbag. Of course, handbags—or pocketbooks—went on being made out of cloth and leather and exotic animal skins (lizard, alligator, even zebra), but by 1950 the new Lucite bag, as it was sometimes called, was a big success. It was sleek, it was clean, and for a short time it was classy. Old-fashioned was out and "modern" was in—given a boost by the 1939 World's Fair, put on hold by World War II, and now back in full force. Cars and appliances were increasingly "futuristic"; middle-class homes were disposing of "traditional" decor in favor of "Danish modern"; and plastic seemed like a magical boon rather than the tacky (and nonbiodegradable) substance it has since come to seem. In 1950, sporting a plastic pocketbook was an easy, highly visible way for a woman to look up-to-date, even fashionable. Besides, these bags were being promoted as practical, though what can have seemed practical about such hard-edged, heavy, and noisy containers is difficult to grasp. On the other hand, in 1950, nobody—not their manufacturers, not their purchasers, certainly not observers of fashion—recognized these bags as the wildly imaginative, even beautiful objects they are beginning to appear to us today. They were new and they were fun, but they weren't *serious*—compared, say, to the latest elegant leatherwork imported from Florence or Rome. Postwar, after all, was a time when almost everything taken seriously in fashion, art, or thought came from abroad; this was the moment of the New Look and Italian neorealism, of existentialism and "The Cocktail Party."

The plastic handbag didn't spring in one creative burst from the mind of a single designer or manufacturer in the nineteen forties. To begin with, it had a few direct ancestors from the twenties and thirties—bags fashioned out of various hard substances: Bakelite, horn, tortoiseshell. (The handbag on page 2 is ca. 1925.) And plastics were already coming into their own before and during the war. There was a natural progression, as people working in, and marketing, plastic began to find new uses for their product. Harry Senzer's career is typical in this regard. Mr. Senzer worked eleven years for a company called Associated Plastics that after the war began making parts for standard cloth or leather handbags—handles, zipper pulls, ornaments, clasps—that Associated would sell to different handbag manufacturers, each of whom was searching for a new look, a new accent. The next step was an entire frame made out of Lucite or Plexiglas (which are more or less the same clear material). These frames held fronts and backs made out of cloth or beading (pages 23, 80, 115). By 1950 there were numerous simple box-shaped bags on the market made completely from transparent Lucite, either colorless or tinted. Then came acetate, which could be made to simulate tortoiseshell because it could be stained and given a high polish, and the classic plastic bag was born. It was about this time that Harry Senzer left Associated Plastics and went to work for a manufacturer called Rialto, who soon brought out its first plastic model. It wholesaled for nine dollars and, according to Senzer, "took off like wildfire." Very quickly Rialto was making dozens of different models, many of them identifiable by their distinctive button-like catch (pages 45, 91). The plastic handbag had become a principal part of its business.

By this time, Rialto's major rivals—Llewellyn (makers of Lewsid Jewels), the elegant Wilardy (originally Handbag Specialties), Myles, Maxim, Charles S. Kahn, Gilli Originals, Florida

Handbags, and Patricia of Miami—were also experimenting with materials, colors, shapes, designs, ornaments, and manufacturing methods. During the nineteen fifties, hundreds upon hundreds of different styles were created. Each season demanded a new look, perhaps up to thirty or forty new designs per manufacturer, and each design might be carried out in half a dozen colors—tortoiseshell, butterscotch, pearl, mink, ivory, gray, black. The manufacturers were certainly inventive, but they also kept a careful eye on each other; clearly, a good deal of that sincerest form of flattery—imitation—was in the air. Rialto actually got out an injunction against one rival who was knocking off a patented design, though no doubt Rialto too was capable of recognizing a good thing when it saw it. (One blatant example of an "imitated" design is the "beehive" on page 119, which one comes across in plastics of various degrees of quality, manufactured by companies of various degrees of honesty. In a November 1951 ad in *Handbags and Accessories*, the industry's trade magazine, Llewellyn boldly claims, "We create and originate all our designs, and protect these designs by U.S. patents"—a headline strategically placed directly above a drawing of the embattled beehive.)

Most handbag manufacture was taking place in the New York area, but as the popularity of the bags spread to Florida in particular, at least one major operation came to flourish there. This was run by Morty Edelstein, who had previously been the "Mor" half of Fre-Mor (Fre-Mor was responsible for the beaded bags mentioned earlier) and then became a partner in Llewellyn before taking over Miami Handbags, to which he added another line, Patricia of Miami. (Patricia, not surprisingly, is Mrs. Edelstein.) It was not only the climate and the Miami market (including a brisk trade with Cuban and South American tourists) that attracted Edelstein to Florida. Labor was undoubtedly cheaper there, and—more important—you could legally use a nitrate substance that was banned in the north. Nitrate—unlike the acrylics and acetates used in New York—was highly flammable; not in the half-inch sheets that would be laminated together, cut out into pieces, softened in hot oil, and bent into the required shapes, but as the original sheets were actually being cut. There were dangerous sparks then, and indeed in 1956 a fire from nitrate shavings swept the Patricia factory—a huge sudden blaze that grew so swiftly there was no time to back out the trucks that were blocking the factory entrance: seventy or eighty people had to crawl out under them. (The fire was so intense that the building's steel beams were bent out of shape.)

Edelstein's bags, displayed throughout this book, have a highly distinctive look, an air of fantasy, partly due to their mottled and marbleized yellows and greens, their distinctive shapes, and their curlicue clasps, but also to the many exotic design elements— threads, stars, sprinkles (the "Mardi Gras" look), foil, leaves—that were pressed between the sheets of nitrate and laminated together to make up the basic walls of his handbags.

Indeed, most of the manufacturers, despite their imitative ways, had their own distinctive design features. Tyrolean specialized in metal filigree (pages 61, 67). Wilardy—makers of the dressiest, most expensive bags—used highly baroque metal clasps (pages 66, 73, 108, 110) and pioneered the application of rhinestones and colored glass (pages 16, 49, 96). Llewellyn (Lewsid Jewel) often lined its very solid bags with heavy silk, partly because many of them opened along the sides rather than at the top and needed a lining to hold them together. Most of the manufacturers employed solid transparent plastic lids, which were etched with an amazing variety of designs— out of leaves, vines, flowers, stars, diamonds, etc. These were hand-carved, then hand-processed on machines, and here again a great deal of "imitation" took place. But the results were extraordinarily hand-some—and grew more and more complicated as ornaments came to be attached to the surface of the lids (gold-plated bees, for instance, were added to the tops of the famous beehive). This, in fact, seems to be the basic pattern: with every season, the manufacturers (presum-ably reacting to their customers) strove for more and more original and complex effects. The sleek, clean surface of the early bags grew encrusted with a variety of materials: rhinestones, colored glass, shells, mirrors, metal strips, metallic ribbon. Shapes grew more and more outlandish: instead of the simple box or oval came trapezoids, triangles, pyramids. There were bags that suggested camel saddles, reliquaries, lunch pails, pagodas, toolboxes, bow ties. (Consider the gray coffin on page 105, complete with fake flowers under its clear dome.) Surfaces became nacreous or luminescent. There were bags imitating cut glass (pages 17, 52, 83), some of them punctuated with large rhinestones. There were bags that revolved within their handles (pages 51, 78), and bags in several layers (pages 59, 74). There were bags with compacts and cigarette cases attached, and bags sold with matching radios or shoes or belts. Stores began special-ordering bags with customers' initials. Some of the higher quality bags were selling in Saks Fifth Avenue or Burdines, in Miami, for seventy or eighty dollars—and these were 1950s dollars. By the late fifties many of the new styles were truly eccentric and even less practical than those of four or five years earlier: With how many outfits could a woman carry a gray coffin? With overspecialization came decline.

There were other contributing factors to this decline, one of which involved the evolving perceptions of the customer. Harry Senzer's wife, Norma, was a buyer of handbags—first in Miami, then for a store called Burnetts in the heart of New York's theater district. (She and Harry first met in the Rialto showrooms.) At first, she says, the plastic bag was tremendously popular with actresses, show people, expensive call girls. "It was a very flashy kind of bag in the beginning," she says. And then its popularity spread and everybody wanted one. But as the up-market versions grew more ornate and more expensive, manufacturers began selling less costly versions too, made out of a much flimsier, cheaper, and more breakable plastic, and from injection molds rather than out of parts pieced together as before. These new bags could be bought for as little as $1.98, and, according to Mrs. Senzer, they speeded up the demise of the quality product. What woman would spend fifty dollars for a bag that closely resembled a three-dollar one molded out of polystyrene? (She calls this the trickle-down theory of fashion.)

Finally, the discovery of vinyl and other pliable substances enabled manufacturers to get around a fundamental disadvantage of the quality hard plastic bag—its weight. Some of these bags (like the gray Llewellyns on pages 31 and 92) are, even empty, so solid and heavy that they're more like weapons than accessories. For daily use, women wanted large, capacious bags, and these were impractical in the heavy acrylics and acetates of the fifties. Vinyl was even more modern than Lucite and acetate—and even shinier!—and it was *light*. Some other materials were light too—like wicker and canvas and thin wooden panels. Suddenly the old plastics must have seemed clunky, clumsy, *old-fashioned*. One can chart their decline by their disappearance from the pages of *Handbags and Accessories*. Throughout the 1950s they're featured and advertised in almost every issue; in 1960 they're practically gone.

The vogue for plastic bags lasted only about a dozen years, but while it lasted, women of almost every social stratum wore them: call girls, yes, but also Clare Boothe Luce, who still was carrying hers recently, as we see in a photograph reproduced several months ago in *The New York Times*; ladies who shopped in Bergdorf's, but also teenagers at Ricky Nelson concerts; New Yorkers and Floridians, of course, but also—as the evidence of countless flea markets and vintage-clothing stores goes to prove—through the midwest and south and New England. One can see them in films of the period, such as *The Human Jungle*, 1954, starring Jan Sterling and Gary Merrill, and *Private Hell 36*, a 1954 Don Siegel movie starring Ida Lupino, Steve Cochran, and Dorothy Malone. And they're still emerging from people's closets and attics: the mothers of three friends of mine have recently and generously disgorged specimens for me. In fact, in the last several years they have been reborn as a fashion article—both as accoutrements for fifties parties and reunions (often they're rented for the occasion from vintage-clothing stores), and as chic accessories to be carried in discos and clubs. Strangest of all, they are now greatly admired (and very expensive) in England, Italy, and Japan; English *Vogue* recently featured a nice but unextraordinary bag that was on sale in London for £143, or well over $200, and shoppers from Rome can be seen hunting them down in SoHo and Miami Beach. Here is one product from America's imperial years that is making its overseas mark thirty-five years late.

What is the aesthetic appeal of these objects today? Their eccentricity, certainly: a kind of unself-conscious inventiveness that is clearly prepared to go all the way, yet is constrained by practicalities. As with Hollywood's golden-age films—westerns or musicals or gangster pictures—one salutes them for their countless ingenious solutions to the question of how to keep reinventing and finding new appeal in a genre that has fundamental rules and demands that can't be ignored. When the rules changed (as happened to Hollywood too, and at about the same time), the genre died.

There's something both sophisticated and naïve about these shapes, these weird combinations of color and material, these occasional lunacies. As pure objects they can dazzle; that becomes instantly clear in the glamorous yet honest photographs taken of the 92 bags in this book by Frank Maresca and Ed Shoffstall. Yes, the bags have been carefully situated and lit and highlighted, but this is what they really look like—if you really look. They turn out, under inspection, to be small-scale architectures, no less elaborate and decorative when taken together than, say, the massed architectures of the Brighton Pavilion. Together, they reflect an energetic design moment when anything could be tried—not by "artists" but by craftsmen and merchants. And, of course, they were not made merely for show. Their other crucial aspect—the thing that makes them so touching, even moving, in conjunction with their extreme style—is that at one time each of them was a highly personal, even intimate, domestic object. They were *used*. Women carried lipsticks and compacts and keys and photographs and handkerchiefs in them; bought them to go with particular dresses or coats; carried them to dinners and parties and theaters; and cared enough about them to store them away in closets and dresser drawers for three decades, certainly without suspecting that one day they would be worth so many lire or yen. These objects, made in vast quantities for profit, bought and used as fashion and for convenience, superseded and forgotten, have turned if not into high art, into high artifact. Although they are clearly related in design to the cars and appliances of their day, they also seem peculiarly related to *our* day, in a way that Cadillac tail fins and avocado washing machines don't. There's some kind of aesthetic relationship between these plastic handbags at their most extreme and the postmodern buildings of the past half-dozen years. Is it reasonable to speculate that in some odd manner, Llewellyn and Wilardy and Rialto and Patricia of Miami anticipate and validate our reactions to Philip Johnson, Robert Venturi, and Robert A. M. Stern? In both cases, the attempt is being made to marry the unrestrainedly bizarre to the requirements of daily life, and perhaps this resemblance explains why—unlike the radios and cars and toasters of their period—these handbags don't really seem dated or nostalgic. Rather, they seem either to have sprung from a moment in our past that lies outside design chronology or to be turning up in antique malls and flea markets all over America from outer space, like the pods in the 1956 *Invasion of the Body Snatchers* (Don Siegel again). And, indeed, can it be that Dana Wynter isn't actually carrying one? A solid Lewsid Jewel could have done major damage to the pod people if wielded properly.

I first bought one of these handbags eight or nine years ago—it was just another peculiar object that caught my eye in an antique/junk store. A year or two later I bought another one. When, a year after that, I came upon a half-dozen more at a flea market, it struck me that here was the stuff of a remarkable collection. There was clearly great variety; the objects involved were utterly startling (this was before they had begun to surface everywhere); the hunt would take me out of the office and into endless shops, malls, fairs, markets, even homes; and the prices were right. At that time, you could buy a good bag for fifteen or twenty dollars, an exceptional one for more, but not a lot more. Of course, I knew nothing about the bags then—where they came from, who used them, how popular they had once been. People selling them only stated that they were "fifties," which was the trendy decade at that time; "it's from the fifties" was the pitch. (Some people said they were "deco," but they said that about Fiestaware too.)

If one is obsessive, and makes the time, a collection can grow fairly quickly, and this one did—through weekend flea markets in and around New York, jaunts to flea markets further afield, and finally expeditions to various cities for various purposes, always including a campaign in vintage-clothing stores and antique malls. In most American cities, people who run such places know and like each other, so that one store owner is likely to send you along to another with the same tastes, and so on. That's how I made my way through such different cities as Miami Beach and Columbus, Ohio—depending on the kindness of strangers.

Today things are somewhat different. Twenty dollars is a bargain price—good bags run forty or fifty dollars, and there are stores where they may be marked at a hundred, or much higher. (Those aren't prices I like to pay.) But as the bags have grown more visible and more valuable, more of them have gone on sale, supply following demand. If one is assiduous, there are still countless models, colors, mutations to be found. A problem more pressing than acquiring them is displaying them. Twenty or thirty are manageable; five hundred, which is about the size of the collection as I write, is hopeless. I keep them now on glass shelves around my bedroom, on bookshelves in halls, on the floor, under my bed. Since my wife doesn't totally grasp the charm of this collection, she shares the bed but leads the waking hours of her home life outside our bedroom.

By far the most serendipitous encounter of my collecting life was brought about by Thelma Wolk, an impassioned antique dealer from Pittsburgh. She and I met first at a New York Pier Show, and the following year she introduced me to Frank Maresca, who, moments before, had bought a plastic bag from her. In five minutes Frank and I had agreed to join forces (and eventually collections). He loved the bags and was planning a large display of them at the Armory show; and by a ridiculous coincidence, Frank—who is both a fashion photographer and a dealer in American primitive art—was already working on a folk art book for Knopf, the publishing house I had recently ceased presiding over. We had never met at Knopf but happily agreed to become collaborators on this book when my old friend and colleague Vicky Wilson, who was already Frank's editor, proposed it.

Frank's colleagues Ed Shoffstall, the photographer, and Lex Boterf have been crucial to the book. Lex pursued the history and data of the bags with the same obsessive determination and thoroughness with which true collectors collect. It was she who tracked down Mr. and Mrs. Harry Senzer, of Rialto, and Mr. Morty Edelstein, of Patricia of Miami, whose interviews have helped us immensely. (Lex carried out the Senzer interview; I was fortunate enough to meet Mr. Edelstein in Miami.) It was also Lex who discovered (at the New York Public Library) and ransacked the back files of *Handbags and Accessories,* fount of much of our knowledge. Also helpful with our research was Carey Pullen.

I want to thank my ex-colleagues at Knopf: Iris Weinstein, who designed this book, Ellen McNeilly, who supervised its production, Nancy Clements, Antoinette White, and, of course, Vicky Wilson; they've all coped gallantly with more interference from an author than anyone needs on such a project. Also, thank you to the dozens of friends who have contributed to the collection. I couldn't possibly cite them all but must single out Jane and Michael Stern, Andrew Vachss, and Rochelle Udelle, for service above and beyond the call of duty. Most of all, loving thanks to Martha Kaplan, who, despite a certain ambivalence toward these artifacts, has staunchly accompanied me to countless places in search of them.

ROBERT GOTTLIEB

PLATES

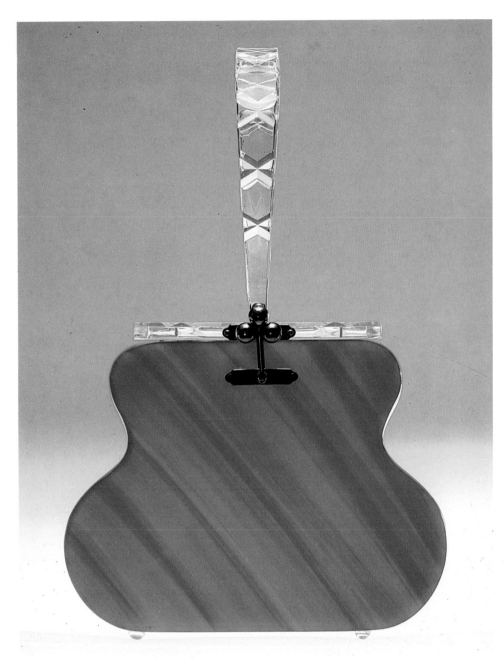

Florida Handbags, ca. 1955–56, 8″ W × 12″ H × 4″ D.

Wilardy, ca. 1954–55, 7$^1/_4$″ W × 9$^1/_2$″ H × 2$^1/_4$″ D.

Llewellyn, ca. 1953–55, 6^1/$_2$″ W × 10″ H × 4^1/$_2$″ D.

Patricia of Miami, ca. 1954–56, 7¹⁄₄″ W × 8″ H × 6″ D.

Lewsid Jewel by Llewellyn, ca. 1951–52, 8″ W × 10¹/₄″ H × 4″ D.

Dorset Rex, ca. 1958, 7¼″ W × 11″ H × 7¼″ D.

Toro, ca. 1954–58, 7¹/₄″ W × 9¹/₄″ H × 3¹/₄″ D.

Frame by Jewel Plastics, insert by Fre-Mor, ca. 1950, 6″ w × 7″ h × 4″ d.

Lewsid Jewel by Llewellyn, ca. 1951–53, 7″ W × 9¹/₂″ H × 4³/₄″ D.

Possibly Gilli Originals, ca. 1952–54, 7″ W × 10¹/₂″ H × 4″ D.

Gilli Originals, ca. 1951–54, 6″ w × 10″ h × 6″ d.

Wilardy, ca. 1955–57, 7¹/₂″ W × 9″ H × 5¹/₂″ D.

Maxim Originals, ca. 1950–55, 6¹/₂″ W × 14″ H × 5¹/₄″ D.

Myles Originals, ca. 1952, 10³/₄″ W × 6¹/₂″ H × 3″ D.

Lewsid Jewel by Llewellyn, ca. 1955, 7^1/$_2$″ W × 11″ H × 3^1/$_2$″ D.

Ranhill, "The Beachcomber," ca. 1954, 7$^1/_2$" W × 11" H × 5$^1/_4$" D.

Llewellyn, ca. 1953–56, 5″ w × 10″ h × 5¹/₂″ d.

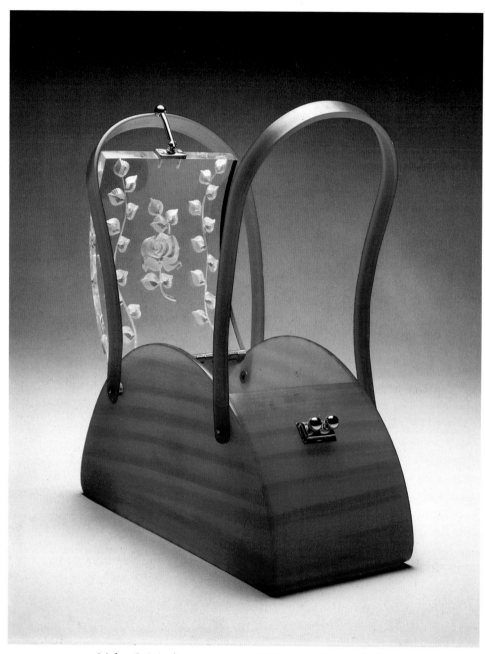

Myles Originals, ca. 1951–53, 8¹⁄₄″ W × 9″ H × 3³⁄₄″ D.

Wilardy, ca. 1954, 7″ W × 8″ H × 5″ D.

Rialto, "Pagoda," ca. 1952, 6¹/₂″ W × 11¹/₂″ H × 5″ D.

Patricia of Miami, ca. 1954–57, 7¹⁄₄″ W × 7¹⁄₄″ H × 4¹⁄₄″ D.

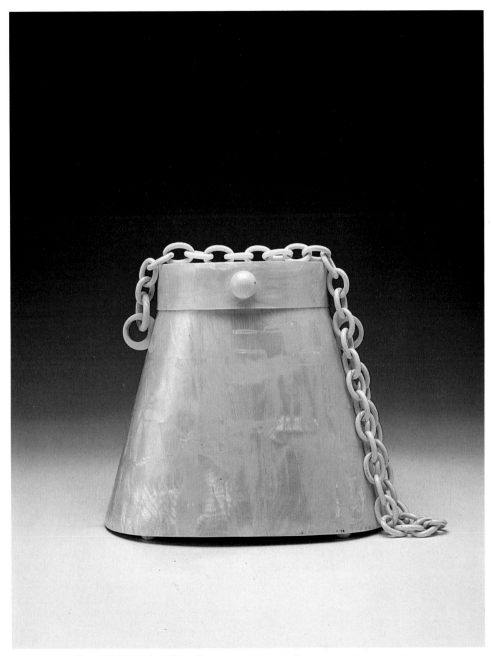

Lewsid Jewel by Llewellyn, ca. 1951, 6³/₄″ W × 5³/₄″ H × 4¹/₂″ D.

Gilli Originals, ca. 1953–54, 7″ W × 12″ H × 5″ D.

Myles Originals, ca. 1954–55, 9¹/₄″ W × 9¹/₄″ H × 2³/₄″ D.

Florida Handbags, ca. 1955–57, 6¹/₂″ W × 11″ H × 4″ D.

Llewellyn, ca. 1951, 8^1/$_2$″ W × 12^1/$_2$″ H × 2^1/$_2$″ D.

Possibly Llewellyn, ca. 1952–53, 10″ W × 8″ H × 4″ D.

Rialto, ca. 1954–56, 6¹⁄₂″ W × 9¹⁄₂″ H × 4″ D.

Gilli Originals, ca. 1953–56, 8¹⁄₄″ W × 9¹⁄₄″ H × 4¹⁄₄″ D.

Llewellyn, ca. 1953–55, 8³/₄″ W × 11″ H × 4¹/₄″ D.

Wilardy, ca. 1952–54, 7″ W × 9¹/₂″ H × 4¹/₄″ D.

Myles Originals, ca. 1951–54, 9¹/₂″ W × 7¹/₂″ H × 3⁷/₈″ D.

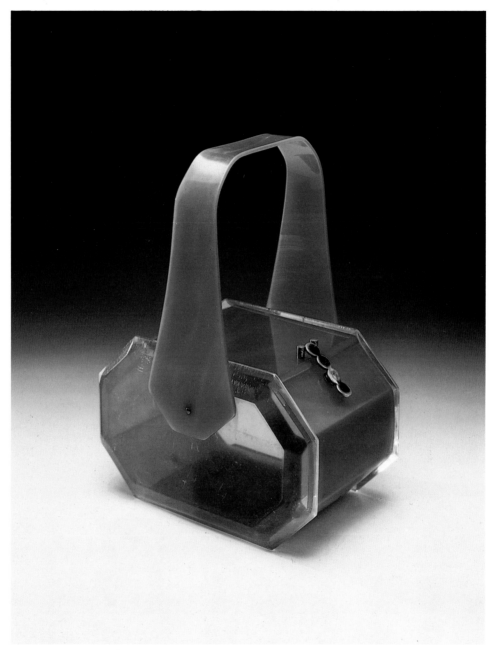

Unknown maker, ca. 1952–55, 7¼″ W × 9½″ H × 5″ D.

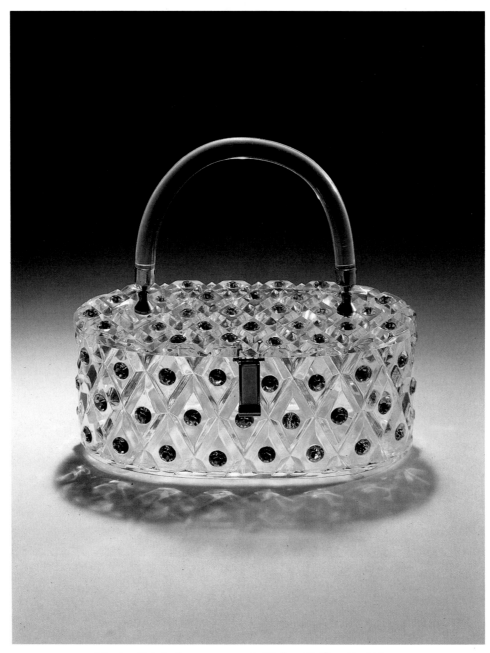

Maxim Originals, ca. 1953–56, 8¹⁄₂″ W × 8″ H × 4¹⁄₂″ D.

Llewellyn, ca. 1954–55, 7³/₄″ W × 10″ H × 5″ D.

Rialto, ca. 1951–56, $6^{1}/_{2}''$ W × $9''$ H × $6^{1}/_{2}''$ D.

Jana, ca. 1954–58, 7$\frac{1}{4}$″ W × 10″ H × 4$\frac{1}{2}$″ D.

Wilardy, ca. 1954, 7^1/$_2$″ w × 9″ h × 4^1/$_2$″ d.

Benne, ca. 1952, 8″ W × 8¹/₂″ H × 3⁷/₈″ D.

Wilardy, ca. 1954, 5³/₄″ W × 9¹/₂″ H × 4³/₄″ D.

Rialto, ca. 1952, 8″ W × 9″ H × 3¹/₂″ D.

Tyrolean, ca. 1951, 8″ W × 10″ H × 4″ D.

Llewellyn, ca. 1955–57, 7¹/₂″ W × 11¹/₄″ H × 2¹/₄″ D.

Myles Originals, ca. 1952, 8″ W × 8¹/₂″ H × 4″ D.

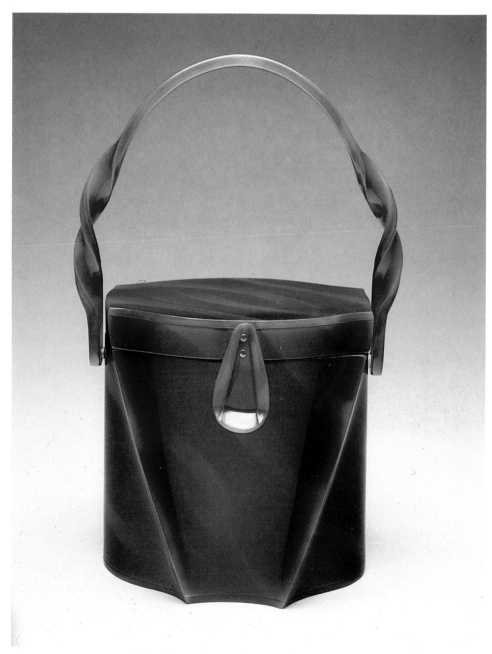

Wilardy, ca. 1954, 6″ W × 11″ H × 4½″ D.

Wilardy, ca. 1955–58, 8³/₄″ W × 11″ H × 3¹/₂″ D.

Tyrolean, ca. 1953–57, 6³/₄″ W × 12″ H × 4″ D.

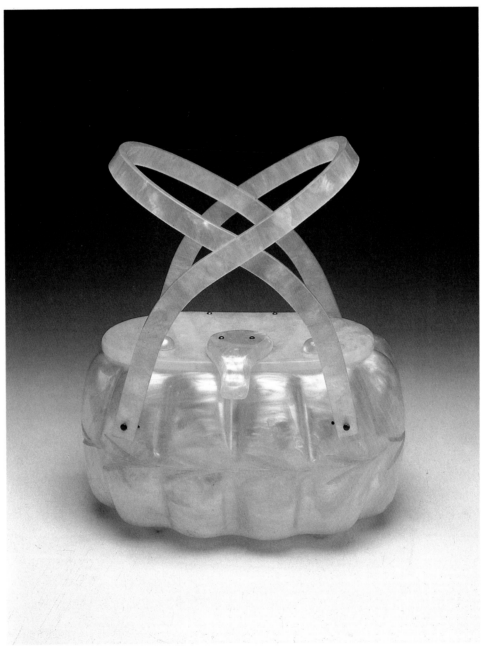

Llewellyn, ca. 1952–54, 7″ W × 10″ H × 5″ D.

Possibly Llewellyn, ca. 1951, 6¹/₂″ W × 11″ H × 5″ D.

Patricia of Miami, ca. 1953–54, 11″ W × 4¹/₂″ H × 2¹/₂″ D.

Lewsid Jewel by Llewellyn, ca. 1951–52, 5³/₄″ W × 10¹/₄″ H × 4″ D.

Wilardy, ca. 1958–59, 6¹/₂″ W × 9¹/₄″ H × 4³/₄″ D.

Wilardy, ca. 1951, 6³/₄″ w × 10″ h × 3¹/₂″ d.

Patricia of Miami, ca. 1953–54, 10″ W × 9″ H × 3⅝″ D.

Wilardy, "Rocket," ca. 1953, 9″ w × 7³/₄″ h × 4¹/₂″ d.

Unknown maker, ca. 1953–56, 7″ W × 8¹/₂″ H × 5″ D.

Gira, ca. 1953–55, 6″ W × 9¹/₄″ H × 4″ D.

Frame by Jewel Plastics, insert by Fre-Mor, ca. 1950, 10³/₄″ W × 9″ H × 3″ D.

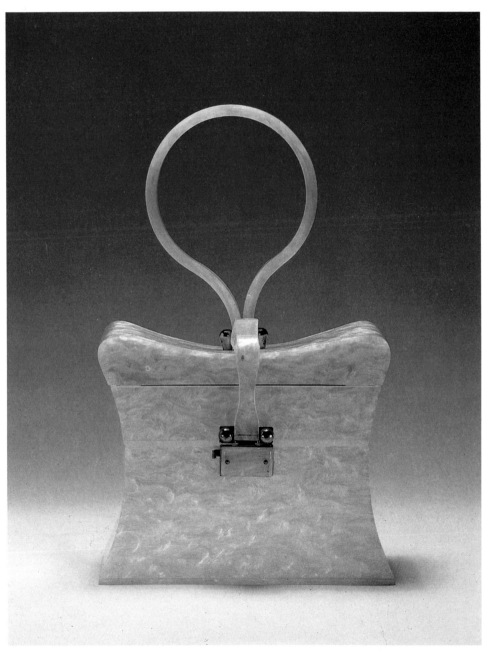

Wilardy, ca. 1950, 7¹/₂″ W × 11¹/₂″ H × 3³/₈″ D.

Unknown maker, ca. 1952–58, 9″ W × 9″ H × 4″ D.

Florida Handbags, ca. 1955–59, 10¹/₄″ W × 7″ H × 4¹/₄″ D.

Myles Originals, ca. 1953–55, 7″ W × 9¹⁄₂″ H × 7″ D.

Rialto, ca. 1951–53, 7″ W × 11″ H × 5″ D.

Wilardy, ca. 1954, 6″ W × 11″ H × 4¼″ D.

Wilardy, ca. 1954–55, 7⁵/₈″ W × 9¹/₂″ H × 4¹/₄″ D.

Rialto, ca. 1952–55, 6³/₄″ w × 9″ h × 4³/₄″ d.

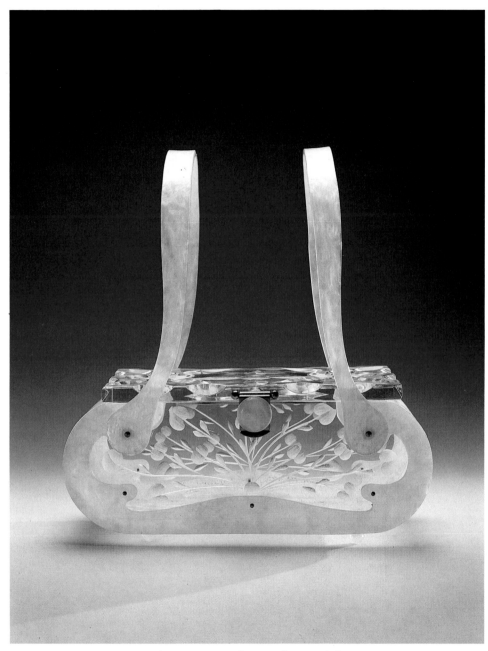

Rialto, ca. 1957, 9″ w × 9″ h × 3¾″ d.

Lewsid Jewel by Llewellyn, ca. 1951–54, 7¹⁄₂″ W × 14¹⁄₂″ H × 4″ D.

Myles Originals, ca. 1951, 6¹/₂″ W × 9″ H × 3¹/₂″ D.

Charles S. Kahn, ca. 1957–59, 6″ W × 9³/₄″ H × 5¹/₂″ D.

Wilardy, ca. 1956, 6″ W × 11″ H × 2¹/₄″ D.

Florida Handbags, ca. 1955–57, 8″ W × 8¼″ H × 5″ D.

Patricia of Miami, ca. 1954–57, 6¹/₄″ W × 10¹/₂″ H × 4¹/₂″ D.

Patricia of Miami, ca. 1954–57, 9³/₄″ W × 9″ H × 4¹/₄″ D.

Possibly Florida Handbags, ca. 1954–57, 8″ W × 7″ H × 5″ D.

Unknown maker, ca. 1954–57, 8″ W × 10″ H × 4″ D.

Rialto, ca. 1959, 6$^{1}/_{2}''$ W × 9$^{1}/_{2}''$ H × 5″ D.

Patricia of Miami, ca. 1954–57, 7³/₄″ W × 9″ H × 6″ D.

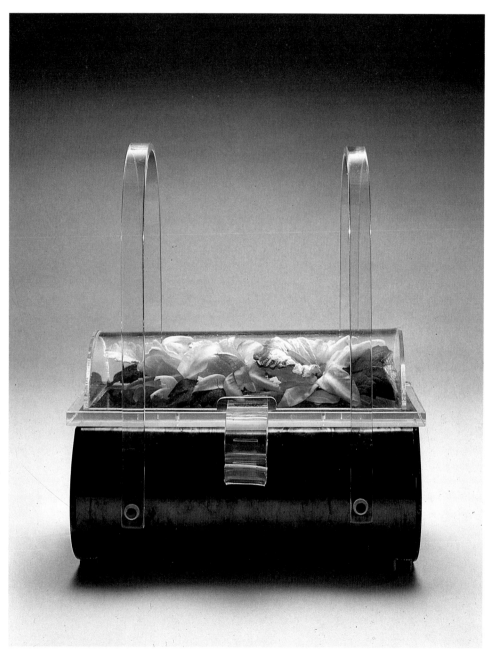

Possibly Harry Litwin, ca. 1954, 7^1/$_2$″ W × 8^1/$_4$″ H × 4^3/$_4$″ D.

Unknown maker, ca. 1951–53, 6⁵/₈″ W × 8″ H × 3¹/₂″ D.

Possibly Dorset Rex, ca. 1953–57, 5³/₄″ W × 8″ H × 6″ D.

Wilardy, ca. 1956, 6¹/₂″ W × 10¹/₂″ H × 3¹/₂″ D.

Toro, ca. 1952–54, 7″ W × 10″ H × 4″ D.

Wilardy, ca. 1959, 9″ W × 10¹/₂″ H × 4¹/₄″ D.

Wilardy, ca. 1954–56, 7¹/₄″ W × 7″ H × 4″ D.

Possibly Myles Originals, ca. 1952–55, 8″ W × 6¹/₂″ H × 2¹/₂″ D.

Patricia of Miami, ca. 1954–57, 6″ W × 10¹/₂″ H × 4¹/₂″ D.

Frame by Jewel Plastics, beaded handle by Fre-Mor, ca. 1950, $6^{1}/_{2}''$ W $\times$ $5^{1}/_{2}''$ H $\times$ $5^{1}/_{2}''$ D.

Charles S. Kahn, ca. 1952–55, 11$^1/_2$″ W × 5″ H × 3$^3/_4$″ D.

Charles S. Kahn, ca. 1955–59, 10″ W × 10¹/₂″ H × 5¹/₄″ D.

Lewsid Jewel by Llewellyn, ca. 1951, 7″ W × 10″ H × 5¹/₂″ D.

A NOTE ON THE TYPE

The text of this book was set in a digitized version of Bembo, a well-known
Monotype face. Named for Pietro Bembo, the celebrated Renaissance writer and
humanist scholar who was made a cardinal and served as secretary to Pope Leo X,
the original cutting of Bembo was made by Francesco Griffo of Bologna
only a few years after Columbus discovered America.

Sturdy, well-balanced, and finely proportioned, Bembo is a face
of rare beauty, extremely legible in all of its sizes.

Composed by The Sarabande Press, New York, New York
Printed and bound by Arti Grafiche Amilcare Pizzi, S.p.A., Milan, Italy
Designed by Iris Weinstein